The Power of Their Voices

Biblical Women Speak

Patricia Ramsden

&

Parson's Porch Books
www.parsonsporchbooks.com

The Power of Their Voices: Biblical Women Speak
ISBN: Softcover 978-1-949888-27-0
Copyright © 2018 by Patricia Ramsden

The Power of Their Voices

Contents

Preface

MANY OF THE STORIES OF WOMEN in the Bible have been sadly neglected. These imaginative interpretations of just a few of these remarkable characters give even familiar stories a fresh perspective and allows the listener to enter into their reality in a different way, bringing them to life once more. They allow us to capture the emotions of these very different women as we rediscover the eternal truths of faith and love, betrayal and grief, victories and defeats.

Chancel drama need not be intimidating. It can be as elaborate or as simple as you like. These narratives have been performed as one woman playlets complete with costuming to sermons delivered from the pulpit while wearing just a simple scarf as a headdress.

The sermons can also be used as the springboard for a group Bible study or a discussion on the roles of the characters in their own time as well as similarities and differences with our lives and times. Such groups do not need to be limited by gender as these narratives will touch the hearts and minds of both men and women with a deeper understand of their lives and the role they played in God's story of love and grace.

Enjoy!

The Rev. Dr. Patricia Ramsden

Eve: Mother of All That Is Living

Genesis 3: 1-20 (RSV)

Now the serpent was more crafty than any other wild animal that the Lord God had made. He said to the woman, 'Did God say, "You shall not eat from any tree in the garden"?' The woman said to the serpent, 'We may eat of the fruit of the trees in the garden; but God said, "You shall not eat of the fruit of the tree that is in the middle of the garden, nor shall you touch it, or you shall die."' But the serpent said to the woman, 'You will not die; for God knows that when you eat of it your eyes will be opened, and you will be like God, knowing good and evil.' So when the woman saw that the tree was good for food, and that it was a delight to the eyes, and that the tree was to be desired to make one wise, she took of its fruit and ate; and she also gave some to her husband, who was with her, and he ate. Then the eyes of both were opened, and they knew that they were naked; and they sewed fig leaves together and made loincloths for themselves.

They heard the sound of the Lord God walking in the garden at the time of the evening breeze, and the man and his wife hid themselves from the presence of the Lord God among the trees of the garden. But the Lord God called to the man, and said to him, 'Where are you?' He said, 'I heard the sound of you in the garden, and I was afraid, because I was naked; and I hid myself.' He said, 'Who told you that you were naked? Have you eaten from the tree of which I commanded you not to eat?' The man said, 'The woman whom you gave to be with me, she gave me fruit from the tree, and I ate.' Then the Lord God said to the woman, 'What is this that you have done?' The woman said, 'The serpent tricked me, and I ate.' The Lord God said to the serpent,

Because you have done this,
  cursed are you among all animals
  and among all wild creatures;
upon your belly you shall go,
  and dust you shall eat
  all the days of your life.
I will put enmity between you and the woman,
  and between your offspring and hers;
he will strike your head,
  and you will strike his heel.'
To the woman he said,
'I will greatly increase your pangs in childbearing;
  in pain you shall bring forth children,
yet your desire shall be for your husband,
  and he shall rule over you.'
And to the man he said,
'Because you have listened to the voice of your wife,
  and have eaten of the tree
about which I commanded you,
  "You shall not eat of it",
cursed is the ground because of you;
  in toil you shall eat of it all the days of your life;
thorns and thistles it shall bring forth for you;
  and you shall eat the plants of the field.
By the sweat of your face
  you shall eat bread
until you return to the ground,

for out of it you were taken;
you are dust,
    and to dust you shall return.'
 The man named his wife Eve, because she was the mother of all
who live.

MY NAME, EVE, MEANS MOTHER of all the living. And yet, ironically enough, through Adam and me came death. You know parts of the story. Hear it now from my perspective as one who lived it and passes it down to you today.

God had created the world in God's own image— the most beautiful place in all the universe, filled with a sense of peace and belonging that was never to be again, until the Lord shall come as the Almighty did then, to walk with us as partners and friends. We called the place "Eden" which means "delight" and that is what it was, our delight — God's delight. The Lord created it all and called it good. Adam and I knew paradise there as no one else has since.

Yet we lost it.

You know the story. Somehow a great evil entered us there in that perfect place — not so much in the form of a serpent but in the desires that were awakened within us — desires to be more than we were, more than we were created to be. For while we were happy there, tending the garden, caring for all living things, there was born in us the temptation to not be satisfied with our role in the world God had made. Instead we wanted to become all that God was and is. It was a need for power — the power to create new worlds apart from the Lord, based solely on ourselves —the power to be in total control of this garden of God's, in total control of ourselves, our fate, our future.

The whispers of the serpent living in our hearts planted a relentless thought, and though we knew we should not desire it, the dream — later to become our nightmare — lived and flourished inside our souls. As we walked with God through creation, as creatures of the Lord's own making, friends of God's own desiring, our secret longing for more grew. We wanted to become gods as well.

The voice of lust and envy, the longing for ultimate power, whispered constantly within us. So when God said we had what we needed to be caretakers of all we could see, our hearts silently cried out, "No. We want more. We want to be more than that, have more than that. We want to possess the earth and do with it what we will."

Those desires snaked silently through our life's blood until the need to make these false dreams a reality overwhelmed us. They overwhelmed our partnership with the Lord and destroyed the companionship, the friendship, we had with the one, the only, true God. So when our creator said that we could have anything in the garden except the knowledge of good and evil, we knew we wanted nothing more than the fruit of that tree even though the Lord told us if we devoured that fruit, if we consumed it, the knowledge would kill something precious inside of us.

Yet still our inner tempters whispered to our hearts, "No. You will not die. You will become like gods, powerful, almighty, worthy of walking with God as God's equal." Surely that is what the Lord would want, we thought, an equal, one who would know the secret of the universe —not a mere caretaker, a subservient friend, determined to carry out God's will.

So when I gazed upon that tree, it became to me the most desirous tree of all, and its fruit promised not death but life in a way we had always longed for life to be but a life that was just beyond our grasp. One day, I was able to withstand it no more. My longing for power outstripped my desire to be faithful, and I gave in to the voices raging inside of me. I consumed the fruit of the one thing that had been denied us — the power to not just play god but to **be** god, the power to know everything, even evil, in all its glory and destructiveness.

That day was truly a day beyond all infamy, a day of disgrace from which we could never turn back. But before the enormity of that moment struck us, we both had been tempted. We both had given in to that voice within ourselves. We knew evil. It was terrifying in its destructiveness. We knew that in that moment we had betrayed ourselves and our God. We had broken more than God's commands. We had broken God's heart and the damage was beyond repair so in our shame we hid from the one who had, until that moment, been everything to our heart and soul — and an eternal, internal war ensued. The battle between the good we longed to do and the wickedness of what we did do raged with no end in sight.

You know that battle, don't you? It's our inheritance to you.

When God came to walk with us that night, we tried to hide the nakedness of our souls. We no longer welcomed God's presence. We dreaded it and what we had become. We knew we had broken the Lord's heart with our sin. Sin. It was the first time that word had a being, a meaning, of its own. And we were afraid —afraid of the One who had made us, who loved us with a never-ending love, afraid of what we had become. We hid ourselves not only from God but from our own selves.

Still, God was faithful and looked tirelessly for us as a mother would search for her missing child. And when the Lord found us, when God saw what we had done, what did we do?

We shifted the responsibility from ourselves to others. We made our actions someone else's fault. Adam blamed me. I blamed the power of the serpent's words inside me. And so, through our own actions, we were banished from the garden where we had once lived in innocent delight, where we discovered the overwhelming temptation to not only have more but to be more.

This — this story — is not just our story. It is yours as well. Take care my child that you too don't give in to the tempting voices whispering in the night. Be strong. Be of great courage. Do not be afraid, for the Lord your God goes with you; the Lord will never leave you nor forsake you. No matter what you do, God will love you and be faithful to you. This is the message of our story — the message of your story — if you only listen and obey.

Sarah: Beautiful, Betrayed, and Barren
Genesis 18: 10-14 (NIV)

Then one of them said, "I will certainly return to you in about a year's time. By then, your wife Sarah will have borne a son." Now Sarah was listening at the tent entrance behind him. Abraham and Sarah were old— really old—and Sarah was beyond the age of childbearing. That's why Sarah laughed to herself, thinking, "After I'm so old and my husband is old, too, am I going to have a child?"

The Lord asked Abraham, "Why did Sarah laugh and think, 'Am I really going to bear a child, since I'm so old?' Is anything impossible for the Lord? At the time set for it, I will return to you— about a year from now—and Sarah will have a son."

ALL RIGHT! SO I LAUGHED! Why shouldn't I laugh? Sarah's going to have a baby! Of course, I laughed. I was 90 years old, and there was God saying that after all these years I would have a son! It was laughable. Besides, why shouldn't I laugh after all those years of being laughed at?

It began right after we were married. "Have you heard?" they'd say, "Sarai can't conceive. Her womb is barren. There will be no baby. Poor Abram. What's he going to do?"

As the years passed, the whispers grew into mocking. "So, Sarai, Abram says he's to be the father of nations, but we haven't seen the first child yet. Shouldn't you be getting started?"

Every day, day in and day out, they'd shout to the world that I was barren and a piece of me would die in shame. But the worst was Abram. I loved him so much, and he loved me, but the future — our future — depended on having sons, and no son ever came.

I remember the first time that God appeared. We were living in Haran then, and God came to Abram in a dream and promised him many descendants. "You will be the Father of nations", the Lord said.

I didn't laugh back then. Instead I believed. I believed that God would give us not just one child but child after child. It was so exciting to live in that time of hope. Every night as I went to bed I would pray that this would be the night, the night I would conceive. But it never happened and slowly but surely all hope died.

Every day I would pray that life would stir inside me. Every day I'd pray that my womb would fill with child. Every day, I'd endure the questions, the whispers, the gossip swirling over my head. Every day I would listen to other children's laughter and to mothers' cooing as they fed their babies at their breasts. Every day a part of me would die.

I don't know what was worse: the scorn from our village or the pity in their eyes. What is a woman worth after all, if she cannot bear a child? I'll tell you what she's worth. Nothing. Nothing at all.

Yet still — Abram loved me. I don't remember a time when he didn't love me. I've always known how much I meant to him, and I knew he never, ever thought that I was worthless.

But I did.

Abram knew how my heart was breaking, and he cared; and so it was to God, and not me, that he cried out his whys, that he cried out for the child I could not have. But still I heard him, and it was as if a knife had been plunged deep into my heart. I wondered when Abram would finally walk away from me, from our home, from our marriage. That's what his friends kept telling him to do.

Finally, the famine came, and with thousands of others, we had to move. We went to Egypt, but Abram was afraid. He was afraid of my beauty and of what the Pharaoh might do, so he asked me to tell them that I was his sister and not his wife, so that they wouldn't kill him to have me.

At first, I couldn't believe what he was saying. I couldn't believe that he would give me away. I felt so betrayed. He kept insisting that he was desperate, that there wasn't another way. "They'd kill me and still have you" he'd say. "Tell them you are my sister, and they will treat me well."

Beautiful. Barren. And Betrayed.

I kept hoping, hope beyond hope, on every step along the way, that Abram would change his tune. That he would fight for me. That he would die rather than subject me to Pharaoh's rape. But nothing happened, and when Pharaoh's men arrived, Abram looked the other way.

It hurt too much to cry. I was alone in my pain, while my husband —my husband —gave me away.

That night, after the Pharaoh was through, I didn't feel beautiful. I didn't feel loved. I felt —- empty, as if I'd gone away inside, as if I would never feel again. And I didn't want to feel anything ever again.

Those were the worst days of my life. I can't begin to speak of them.

Finally, I cried out loud to God, "Why? Why? What have I ever done to deserve this? Please, please help me."

How did I dare to speak to God like that you ask?

I dared, because despite it all, I believed. I believed that God was there. That God cared. That God would help. And God heard, and God saved me.

It was then that I knew I belonged to God just as surely as Abram did. What I discovered in Egypt was that God was with me, even with me, even in the depth of my pain. God cared.

Nothing was ever the same for me again. Once I was nothing, but now I was the beloved child of God's.

And Abram? After God rescued me from the palace, I was sent back to be with Abram. Slowly but surely, I began to forgive.

Still, I was barren. I just didn't dwell on it. I stopped expecting to conceive. But God went on telling Abram that he was blessed, that his descendants would be like the stars in the sky, far too many to count.

When I knew beyond any doubt that I could not conceive, I went to Abram and told him to take my slave, the one we called Hagar, to conceive a child in her. I'm sure people wondered why I hadn't given him a slave before. But the truth is I couldn't bear the thought of it. The night he went to her I cried myself to sleep. In the hours before dawn, Abram came in to hold me tight. "It meant nothing, Sarai," he said. "It's you I love. It's you who I will always love."

But before long, Hagar was with child Abram's child, and her taunts began to torment me. "Why should I obey you?" she'd say. "Who are you to give me orders? I'm the one carrying Abram's child. You are nothing. You will always be nothing."

I made her life miserable. I gave her impossible tasks to do and then punished her for not completing them. Finally, she ran away, and I was glad. But then she came back. This time it was as if she was clutching a secret within her heart.

Slowly the days passed until she bore a son we named Ishmael. I took the child from her breast and pronounced him ours — mine and Abraham's. And so, Abraham had his long-promised son. I tried to love him, truly I did. But I always knew he was not my child, the child of my womb. For me, it was not the same.

Then the angel came again. I was to have a child, a child of my own womb. I laughed. It was impossible. My time for child bearing had come and gone long ago.

Then at long last it happened. Beyond all belief it happened. I was with child. The Lord answered our prayers and gave us a son. At ninety years old, I was to have a son. Oh, it's true. I laughed from the amazement of it — from the sheer joy of it. I was going to be a mother. Isaac would be my son, and I knew, I knew, who our God was. The Lord is the God who makes the impossible possible.

But Ishmael was still there and by the law, he was Abraham's first-born son. Everything would come to him, including the blessing of God. It ate at me like a snake devouring my soul. Finally, I lost all my sound judgement, I lost all my faith, and I insisted Abram get rid of her. "Do what you want," he said. "She doesn't mean anything to me."

So, I sent her away. I banished her from our camp and sent her out to the desert without food or water, knowing that there she and her precious child would die. I've regretted it ever since it happened. I, above all, should have had more compassion. So I asked for God's forgiveness, and once more I found the Lord's grace.

Our God is the God who is with me no matter what I have done. Our God is the God who hears our prayers and responds to them — perhaps not the way we want the Lord to respond — perhaps not when we expect God to — but respond the Lord did and does. God responds with love and concern. Believe, just believe, in this wonderful, powerful God of life, this Lord, who against all odds, kept God's promises to me —and will keep them for you as well.

Hagar: A Slave

Genesis 16 (RSV)

Now Sarai, Abram's wife, bore him no children. She had an Egyptian slave-girl whose name was Hagar, and Sarai said to Abram, 'You see that the Lord has prevented me from bearing children; go in to my slave-girl; it may be that I shall obtain children by her.' And Abram listened to the voice of Sarai. So, after Abram had lived for ten years in the land of Canaan, Sarai, Abram's wife, took Hagar the Egyptian, her slave-girl, and gave her to her husband Abram as a wife. He went in to Hagar, and she conceived; and when she saw that she had conceived, she looked with contempt on her mistress. Then Sarai said to Abram, 'May the wrong done to me be on you! I gave my slave-girl to your embrace, and when she saw that she had conceived, she looked on me with contempt. May the Lord judge between you and me!' But Abram said to Sarai, 'Your slave-girl is in your power; do to her as you please.' Then Sarai dealt harshly with her, and she ran away from her.

The angel of the Lord found her by a spring of water in the wilderness, the spring on the way to Shur. And he said, 'Hagar, slave-girl of Sarai, where have you come from and where are you going?' She said, 'I am running away from my mistress Sarai.' The angel of the Lord said to her, 'Return to your mistress, and submit to her.' The angel of the Lord also said to her, 'I will so greatly multiply your offspring that they cannot be counted for multitude.' And the angel of the Lord said to her,

Now you have conceived and shall bear a son;

you shall call him Ishmael,

for the Lord has given heed to your affliction.

He shall be a wild ass of a man,

with his hand against everyone,

and everyone's hand against him;

and he shall live at odds with all his kin.'

So she named the Lord who spoke to her, 'You are El-roi'; for she said, 'Have I really seen God and remained alive after seeing him?' Therefore, the well was called Beer-lahai-roi; it lies between Kadesh and Bered.

Hagar bore Abram a son; and Abram named his son, whom Hagar bore, Ishmael. Abram was eighty-six years old when Hagar bore him Ishmael.

I AM JUST A SLAVE, a piece of property to be used and abused by those who own me -- not a person, not a human being with rights and dignity. Sarah could not — would not --even call me by name — for to give me a name was to see me as I am — a woman, like her, wanting what is best for my son whom I love.

My name is Hagar and Ishmael is my son. This is my story.

The word throughout the camp was that God had come to visit with Abraham and Sarah and had promised them a son who would be blessed. From Abraham and Sarah, a new covenant would begin, and their descendants would be as numerous as the stars in the sky. But Sarah was barren and bore no son.

Year after year Sarah waited for a child to call her own, a child of the promise. Until finally, in despair, she decided to take matters into her own hands. If she could not have a child from her own womb, she would have a child by another.

She went to Abraham with her plan intact. She would give me to him so that the child I bore would become her child, Abraham's child. And so, it was. Abraham went into me. Such polite language for the rape that took place between a master and his slave.

Still I did not weep. I did not want them to have the power to make me weep and I prayed that I would bear a child, a son, for Abraham — not for Abraham's sake but for the sake of the child himself, for my sake.

Though the rule of law at the time clearly said that such a child born of a slave girl would become the child of the master and his wife, yet still the child would come from me — from my womb. He would inherit my love and my being, and nothing — no law by man — could ever take that away from me. It mattered not what the law said — the child was mine — mine, and yes, Abraham's as well.

The time before the birth of my son, a time which should have been filled with joy and wonder, was filled instead with hardship and pain. Sarah treated me harshly out of her jealousy and Abraham said she could do as she wanted, for I was, in the end, her property. There was no protection for a slave girl and her unborn son. Instead there was task after impossible task for me to do and beatings when I could not complete them. Each day brought new indignities, new sufferings.

Finally, I could take it no more and I ran from our camp into the desert, preferring the desert's harshness over the brutality of my mistress.

But God found me there, and the Lord asked, "From where do you come and where are you going?" I told the Lord God Almighty that I had run from my mistress and I would seek a new life in a different place.

But the Lord said, "No, my child. You must go back." Then God gave to me a promise, a sacred oath, that my child would be blessed and would have children too numerous to count, for the Lord had heard my cries of despair and answered them.

So I returned to camp — and in due time, the child was born. He was the first-born son of Abraham and the promise was with him. He was a beautiful child, a child of the covenant.

Then, the impossible happened. Sarah gave birth to a son as well — a child from her own womb — to carry the promise of God to both Sarah and Abraham. Then Sarah knew.

She watched as Ishmael and Isaac played together, like the brothers they were, and her heart trembled within her for she knew the truth of what would happen. She knew the law. Ishmael was the first-born child. By the law all rights and privileges of the first-born son were to come to him.

So Sarah went to Abraham. "Get rid of that woman and her child. I don't care what it costs, I don't care what you do, just get rid of them. Send them away and let Isaac and Isaac alone inherit God's blessings upon us.

But Abraham's heart was filled with compassion. He could not send us defenseless into the desert's sun and heat to die slowly from lack of food and water. Then God appeared once again and said it was so. It must be done. We must be banished.

Early the next morning, before the heat of the sun, Abraham gave to me a few loaves of bread and a skein of water. Then he sent us out into the desert to die. I took Ishmael by the hand and led him away from the only life he had ever known into a certain death.

We traveled for miles in the hot desert sun. Our food and water were quickly gone. At last there was no more, and the child was growing weaker day by day, hour by hour, begging for me to help him — begging for just a swallow of water.

Ishmael, forgive me. I could take it no more. I could not stand by and watch my child die such a slow and agonizing death. So I left him under the protection of some bushes and I moved away.

Finally, the tears flowed. I began to sob over the tragedy of it all. What had I ever done to deserve such punishment? What had Ishmael done to deserve to die? Why was this our fate? As I sobbed out my grief, the Lord God appeared to me.

We were not to die a desert death. Instead the Almighty said that Ishmael, my Ishmael, would become the father of many nations, just as the Lord had promised so long ago. Water appeared. Food was nearby. We would be spared.

My son grew in stature and strength and he became a tribal leader of many nations — later to be called the Muslims.

All the blessings of God came to pass, but from that day to this Ishmael's tribes and the tribes of Isaac have despised and hated one another with a hatred that comes only from great bitterness.

As you pray this day and in days to come, I ask that you pray for peace in all the lands now occupied — peace for a war-torn area in our world — peace with an understanding that the weapons can at long last be laid down. Please — please — pray for peace for all our nations — your nation — and for all the world.

Leah: Jacob's Wife

Genesis: 29: 16-31(RSV)

Now Laban had two daughters; the name of the elder was Leah, and the name of the younger was Rachel. Leah's eyes were lovely, and Rachel was graceful and beautiful. Jacob loved Rachel; so he said, 'I will serve you seven years for your younger daughter Rachel.' Laban said, 'It is better that I give her to you than that I should give her to any other man; stay with me.' So Jacob served seven years for Rachel, and they seemed to him but a few days because of the love he had for her.

Then Jacob said to Laban, 'Give me my wife that I may go in to her, for my time is completed.' So, Laban gathered together all the people of the place and made a feast. But in the evening, he took his daughter Leah and brought her to Jacob; and he went in to her. (Laban gave his maid Zilpah to his daughter Leah to be her maid.) When morning came, it was Leah! And Jacob said to Laban, 'What is this you have done to me? Did I not serve with you for Rachel? Why then have you deceived me?' Laban said, 'This is not done in our country—giving the younger before the firstborn. Complete the week of this one, and we will give you the other also in return for serving me for another seven years.' Jacob did so and completed her week; then Laban gave him his daughter Rachel as a wife. (Laban gave his maid Bilhah to his daughter Rachel to be her maid.) So Jacob went in to Rachel also, and he loved Rachel more than Leah. He served Laban for another seven years.

When the Lord saw that Leah was unloved, he opened her womb; but Rachel was barren.

LIKE RACHEL, I LOVED HIM from the first time we met, but I knew it was hopeless. How could I dare hope to compete with Rachel? She was everything I wasn't. Beautiful, vivacious, charming. All you had to do was look at Jacob and you knew he only had eyes for her. For seven years he worked for her hand. For seven years I prayed for just one glance from him, one caring look, one opportunity to tell him how I felt. But nothing. I was nothing. Nothing but Rachel's old maid sister, unable to get a man of my own — unattractive, unloved, unwanted. Who did I think I was fooling when I couldn't even fool myself?

So there I was, as Rachel went dancing, spinning around the camp getting ready for her wedding night. She was so happy it was as if she were sparkling every place she went. Nothing bothered her. She couldn't wait to tell me every single detail about the parties and the wedding feast and the drinks being prepared. I fingered the rich cloth of her wedding robes and the veil that would cover her face. I don't think it ever occurred to her that each detail was torture for me.

I was the oldest sister. By all rights my marriage should come first. But who would have me? Who would look twice at me with the beautiful Rachel around? Not even my father's wealth could marry me off.

Then it happened. Suddenly. Shockingly. So suddenly, so shockingly, I could barely take it in. It was the very day of the wedding. Suddenly father was throwing Rachel to the floor of my tent, and she was weeping inconsolably as if her heart were broken never to be mended again.

What was happening? This was the day of her joy, her love. What could possibly cause her so much pain on such a day as this? Then Father commanded me to stay inside, to stay inside and not say a word to anyone — not even the slaves. No one was to see us. Then he left without any explanation. I could hear the party outside the tent as the feasting and drinking went on and on.

When Rachel finally controlled her weeping, she sobbed out to me father's plan. It was not to be her night, but mine. In the robes, with the veils, Jacob would be too drunk to realize what was happening and it would be too dark for him to see which bride he was taking. I was to be given to him without his knowledge, without his desire, without his love.

I knew if I only but spoke to him, there alone in the darkness, he would know I was not Rachel. He would know he was being duped. But I loved him so much. I wanted him so badly. This was my only chance, my one chance, at marriage and happiness, so I did as father asked and I kept silent. Jacob never knew.

Until morning. In the morning, he looked and saw and screamed in rage as he rushed to our Father. I will never forget his words as he cried out in anguish, "What have you done! Why have you deceived me?" I just lay there covered in shame and humiliation. He would never love me. He would never care.

The week that was to be our wedding week was instead a week of hell as Jacob counted the minutes till he could be with the one he really wanted, the one he really loved. Oh, he entered me, but it was more from rage than desire as if he were punishing my body for my father's lies.

But God heard my cries. God knew the love in my heart. So the Lord opened my womb. I was so happy. I knew — I just knew — that if I gave Jacob a son he would come to love me too — oh, maybe not as much as Rachel — never as much as Rachel —but at least some. So I named my son Reuben because God had heard my affliction and at last my Jacob would love me. But it was not to be. Son after son I gave him, sons that would one day become the tribes of Israel, but Jacob never took me except in pity. He never really wanted me, not as a lover or a wife. I was always second best.

But my love never waned. I would take whatever Jacob would give, even if it were just the crumbs left under his table, but for all the love I had for him, a new love — a different kind of love — grew in my heart.

Time after time, Jacob's God heard my cries in the night and the Lord's love enfolded me. The Lord God reminded me of the children I bore and of their love for me as well. Slowly I learned that I, even I, was a woman of value, a woman created to love and be loved, and I took solace in the heart of God and the love of my sons.

I know that to you, my story is not a happy one, not a pleasant one. There is no magical fairy-tale ending. Yet to know that even such as I, the unwanted, unloved wife, could be valued by a God such as Jacob's God, is everything to me. May it become everything to you as well.

Rachel: The Beloved

Genesis 29: 9-18 (RSV)

Rachel arrived with her father's sheep, since she was a shepherdess. When Jacob saw Rachel, the daughter of Laban, his mother's brother, accompanied by Laban's sheep, Jacob approached the well, rolled the stone from the opening of the well, and then watered his mother's brother Laban's flock. Then Jacob kissed Rachel and began to cry out loud. Jacob told Rachel that he was related to her father, since he was Rebekah's son, so she ran and told her father.

When Laban heard the news about his sister's son Jacob, he ran out to meet him. He embraced him, kissed him, and brought him back to his house. Then Jacob told Laban about everything that had happened. Laban responded, "You certainly are my flesh and blood!" So Jacob stayed with him for about a month.

Later, Laban asked Jacob, "Should you serve me for free, just because you're my nephew? Let's talk about what your wages should be. "Now Laban happened to have two daughters. The older one was named Leah and the younger was named Rachel. Leah looked rather plain, but Rachel was lovely in form and appearance. Jacob loved Rachel, so he made this offer to Laban: "I'll serve you for seven years for Rachel, your younger daughter."

It Really Was Love At First Sight. I know. I know. It sounds like something you'd only hear in fairy tales but for us it was true. I'd been watching my father's flocks like any other day and had gone to the well, just like any other day, but then, there he was. Suddenly it was like no other day at all.

We used to laugh because when he saw me, he just stopped and stared for a moment then he ran to the well and lifted off the stone cover in one majestic heave. It usually takes three or four men to just barely shove it off. He told me I would never know how much it cost him to show off those muscles of his!

He didn't have to do it you know. He had me at "hello". Then he gazed in my eyes and kissed me. We never looked back from that first kiss.

He worked for my father for a month before my father asked what he wanted in return for his labor. His answer was certain and strong. "I want Rachel to be my wife."

I was on top of the world until my father hemmed and hawed and finally told him, "You can have her as a bride — but you must work in the fields and pastures for seven years for such a prize." Seven years! Who had ever heard of such a thing! It was far longer than anyone could possibly expect, but Jacob didn't hesitate.

"Seven years then. For Rachel, I'll labor seven years." As we would sit under the stars at night after a long, hot day, Jacob would hold me and say, "I love you so much that even seven years seem like days and each day a year as I wait for us to be together forever."

At times it seemed as if our wedding night would never come, but finally the waiting was over. I will never forget the tragedy of that day that was supposed to be the happiest day of all. There I was in the tent, preparing my robes and the veil that would hide my face when Father entered in.

"Put the robes aside," he ordered. "They are not for you to wear. They are Leah's."

"What? Don't jest with me today, Father. It's finally here. In a few hours I will belong to Jacob."

"No. I have other plans for you — and for Jacob."

"But you can't," I cried. "You promised. You took a vow. For seven years we have waited. Today is the day. The feast is ready."

"I said no. For now, you are still my daughter, my property, and I'll do what I want with you. Jacob shall have a bride alright, but it is to be Leah this night. Not you."

I couldn't believe it. How could he? Why would he? Jacob did not love Leah. He had not labored for Leah. It was for me! All for me! I was the love of his life! But Father gagged me and drug me from the tent. He took me to Leah's, throwing me on her tent's floor, weeping and crying, moaning that this couldn't be.

But it was. Leah went in my place to become Jacob's bride and I wept throughout the night. When morning came I heard his cry of anguish. The entire camp heard his fury as he rushed to my father. "How could you do this? Why would you betray me? I kept my part of the bargain. For seven years I worked without a complaint — and now, now I discover Leah is my reward! Leah! That's no reward! I never wanted Leah! Give me my Rachel. Give her to me now!"

For a moment, I thought he would shed my father's blood over me, but just in time my father promised me to him again — for another seven years of servitude. My heart broke as I waited for Jacob's answer. What man would agree to such a thing? But so strong was his love that he agreed — on the condition that he claim me now even if the marriage must wait.

"At the end of seven days," Father said. "For seven days you are to be with Leah. That is our way."

So it was. At the end of the seven days, Jacob and I joined together, forever. It was not easy — neither for Leah nor me. I had Jacob's love — but she had his sons. For whatever reason, I could not conceive. I begged Jacob. I begged God, but no child filled my womb. Then, finally, it happened. My happiness was complete as life stirred inside me. I bore a son — Jacob's son — his favorite son: Joseph. I knew somehow this child of our love was destined to be special, a favored child not only of Jacob but of God. "Someday," I said, "he will be great and will rule over all his brothers! Someday he will be like the rainbow, a sign of God's promise, wearing a cloak of many colors."

It was a long birth, a difficult birth, but as I lay there in Jacob's arms cradling our Joseph, I would have it no other way. It sounds like a fairy tale. Love conquered all. Nothing could separate us. Love truly is patient and kind. It always protects, always trusts, always hopes, always perseveres. May you come to know that same love that is shared between Jacob and me.

Naomi: Great Grandmother of David

Ruth 4: 13-17 (RSV)

So Boaz took Ruth and she became his wife. When he made love to her, the Lord enabled her to conceive, and she gave birth to a son. The women said to Naomi: "Praise be to the Lord, who this day has not left you without a guardian-redeemer. May he become famous throughout Israel! He will renew your life and sustain you in your old age. For your daughter-in-law, who loves you and who is better to you than seven sons, has given him birth."

Then Naomi took the child in her arms and cared for him. The women living there said, "Naomi has a son!" And they named him Obed. He was the father of Jesse, the father of David.

THEY WERE SUCH HAPPY DAYS. We lived in Bethlehem then. It was a land of peace and prosperity and my life was filled with the love of my husband Elimelech and our two sons. Surely life lived up to the meaning behind my name, Naomi, for it means "all is pleasant in the Lord", and truly my life equaled the name of "My Delight". But then the famine came, and we lost everything. The boys were starving and finally, in desperation, Elimelech decided we must leave or die so we went to build a new life in Moab. But it wasn't long before tragedy struck again.

Elimelech grew sick. Each day was filled with pain, his pain and mine, as I sat helpless, unable to relieve his suffering and make him well again. Finally, he died in my arms, leaving me a grieving widow. But life must go on and day by day my grief lessened in the love and care of our sons and their wives. With the loss of my husband, they became my delight and I found new meaning, a new reason for living, in them. What mother was ever so blessed with such loving sons and devoted daughter-in laws? They cared for me as if I were their own mother and so my love for them grew each day.

But the Lord was not finished with me yet. Just as my beloved Elimelech passed on so did my sons. Each died of the same dreadful sickness that took my beloved Elimelech away from me. Once more I was left with nothing — nothing but the love of Ruth and Orpah. But of what use was their love? They could not give me back my security — or my sons. The pain in my heart was too much to bear, and I cried out to God the eternal question of why. But no answer came.

I longed once more for my life in Bethlehem and all the promises it once held. I longed for the dreams of my youth, even though I knew they had melded into my nightmare of a life never to be again. Still I would be home — home amongst my own people in the land of my God.

So I told Ruth and Orpah that I must leave. I was going home, and they too should return to their homes and their families to build their own lives with a new future and new husbands to love. They had no future with me. I was too old to bear more sons, too old for the hope of a new life. It was what was best — for them and for me.

So I set my face back toward the land of Judah. But both of the girls held on to me weeping and crying "No." My heart broke at their new grief, a grief and a pain caused by me. My anger over my fate lashed out at them with a viciousness that cut like a whip as I insisted that they leave me to build new lives of their own and find new loves.

Finally, Orpah did as I wished, turning her face toward home. However, Ruth, Ruth refused to leave me as she spoke the words of committed love that still ring through the ages whenever love is declared.

I will never forget what she said then in the midst of our mutual grief and sorrow: "Don't urge me to leave you or to turn back from you. Where you go I will go, and where you stay I will stay. Your people will be my people and your God my God. Where you die I will die, and there I will be buried. May the Lord deal with me, be it ever so severely, if even death separates me from you."

And so, we left together.

At last we reached Bethlehem, and as my friends greeted me as the Naomi I once was, full of life and joy, I begged them to call me only by my new name, filled with bitterness, the name of Mara. "I went away full," I told them, "but the Lord has brought me back empty. Why call me Naomi? The Lord has afflicted me; the Almighty has brought misfortune upon me."

But my friends said no. They would not let me stay in my bitterness. They would not call me Mara. Instead they would walk beside me until I was Naomi again.

Slowly, oh so slowly, I began to heal once more through the kindness of my friends and the devotion of Ruth. I found a sort of peace, though not the peace I once knew. Life was hard with no husbands to care for us. We lived in a hovel on some land my husband left me, and we had to depend on the kindness of others for food.

Finally, I heard that Boaz still lived in Bethlehem and my heart stirred. He was a close relative of my Elimelech and I had heard he was a kind man with a good heart, so I sent Ruth to him, begging for a chance to glean the barley left in the fields after the harvesters were done so we would not starve. Of course, he said yes. How could he not?

So Ruth went into the fields. When Boaz saw her there, his heart was filled with her beauty and the gentleness of her nature as well as her steadfast devotion to me. When Ruth returned home after that first day's labor, carrying the barley she had gathered, she told me of the virtues of Boaz, what a kind man he was and how he had taken care of her and ensured she was safe there in the fields alone with his men.

It was then that hope began to be born in my heart again. Perhaps, just perhaps, Boaz might be the answer to my pleas to God. So I told Ruth to return to the fields to catch Boaz's eye and perhaps to catch his heart.

So it was. Boaz loved her and wanted her as his wife.

But there was another who had claim to her and to me, who insisted he must have the land Elimelech had given me. But Boaz reminded him that to have our meager piece of land and our home meant he was to take Ruth as well, a foreigner from Moab and not a Jew. The man was horrified and told Boaz that if he wanted, Boaz could have both the land and the woman.

At last Boaz and Ruth were married. Love reigned in our new home once more, but there was a place in my heart that was still as empty as before. Yet one day, one great and glorious day, that place was filled with content and joy once more, for Ruth placed in my arms her newborn son, my grandson, Jesse, who against all odds, would become the father of David, the great king of Israel, favored by the Lord.

May the name of the Lord be eternally praised. May our household always know peace and God's eternal love forever more.

Mary: The Mother of Jesus

Luke 2: 4-7 (NIV)

So Joseph also went up from the town of Nazareth in Galilee to Judea, to Bethlehem the town of David, because he belonged to the house and line of David. He went there to register with Mary, who was pledged to be married to him and was expecting a child. While they were there, the time came for the baby to be born, and she gave birth to her firstborn, a son. She wrapped him in cloths and placed him in a manger, because there was no guest room available for them.

IT WAS SO LONG AGO, and yet it seems like yesterday. I was surrounded by light and a whisper. Then almost without realizing it, I heard my voice whispering "yes." Yes. A word that would hold all of eternity in its grasp. Time split in half. Before... and after.

I was too young, much too young, to know what yes meant, and yet even now I know I would say yes again. Perhaps not as quickly. Perhaps with tears flowing unchecked. Certainly, with a broken heart.... but still, in the end, yes.

In those early days, when I felt life moving within me, I was filled with wonderment —— and morning sickness. It seems no one ever stops to think of the reality of my life. They have it wrapped up in their imagination, so it seems like a dream, a wonderful dream. But the reality, the reality, was far different. Joseph's anger, my mother's shame, the whispers and stares, the tears in the night and my prayers of why? Why me? Why like this?

Then there was the journey. Nine months pregnant, I could barely move let alone get comfortable on the swaying back and uneven gait of that donkey. Yet hour after hour I rode while Joseph walked alongside, trying to pretend he knew what we were doing, where we were going. Oh, we knew we were traveling to

Bethlehem, but that was not our real destination. We both knew we had no idea where this journey of God's would end.

Looking back on those days now, it almost seems funny. The sort of story you share around the table years after the fact when the family has gathered together to remember and celebrate.

First, there was nowhere to stay so we wound up begging just to spend the night in a cave with the animals, anything for shelter. The pains had already started and neither Joseph nor I knew what would come next. He just kept clutching my hand — or I clutched his. The pains rolled over me coming faster and faster. Neither one of us knew about babies and Joseph was even more terrified than I was. He was a carpenter, not a shepherd, so he'd never even seen a lamb born, let alone a mother sweating and pushing and praying for it to end. I remember Joseph wiping Jesus off and whispering over and over again that He was beautiful, just beautiful, a miracle of a child.

We grew together. Me, Joseph and our child. We became family and there were more babies — brothers and sisters for Jesus to play with and look after, but He was the oldest and so it was He Joseph taught to be a carpenter. When Joseph died before his time, it was Jesus who became the man of the house.

Then, one day, He was gone. Just like that. No looking back. He told me it was His time and I knew it was true. But watching Him walk away broke my heart in a way nothing else could do. I was terrified — terrified for Him and all that lay ahead of Him.

Finally, His brothers went after Him, trying to drag Him home, but His home wasn't really in Nazareth, not anymore, and we were no longer His family. I think it had to be that way or it would have been more than any of us could bear.

Days. Years. They went by in a whirl of miracles and storytelling and teaching us all about love. He talked of God as His Abba, His real Daddy. He spoke of how God longed to become a Daddy for all of us — no exceptions.

That's really how the trouble started. No exceptions. Tax collectors, lepers, rabbis, pharisees. He told us God loved us all — and it was more than some could take.

His popularity grew and grew until it seemed impossible for Him to escape the crowds for even a few hours. Everyone pressed in around Him begging for some kind of healing, physical, emotional, spiritual healing. I stood back and watched and prayed and longed to hold Him close, to protect Him, not just from the enemies He was making, but to protect Him from Himself. It seemed at times that I heard God's voice whispering in my heart, "ahhh but you said yes."

The day He entered Jerusalem I thought my heart would break with joy. For days I believed there would be a wonderful ending to our story. But then the whispering started, the rumors of how Jesus was really a traitor to the faith, a traitor to God, and I began to fear what lay ahead.

I was in the middle of the crowd that day, standing in front of the palace. When they brought Him out, I didn't know who He was — bloodied, bruised, barely able to stand. I started to fall, and Merriam caught me, holding me close as the crowd started to cry "Crucify! Crucify!" "Noooo," I screamed. "Noooo. You don't understand. Why can't you see?" I was hysterical as Merriam fought to hold me back from beating at the crowd, from rushing the palace myself if necessary.

Then Pilate washed His hands and Jesus was led away, stumbling after the guards who thrashed Him forward with their whips as if He were nothing more than a dog, but even a dog they would have put out of his misery.

Instead they kept torturing my Son, my Son, my precious baby boy. I remembered holding Him to my breast and laughing softly as He sucked. I remembered first steps and first words. I remembered when I was frantic because we had lost Him at the temple. I remembered, and each memory was a dagger in my heart.

I stumbled my way to Golgotha. The place reeked with the stench of pain and death. The ground itself was stained red with the blood of countless victims. It was a hill of torture where men went mad and prayed for death long before death would ever come.

I screamed with each pounding of the nails. It took all of the other women to hold me back, to keep the soldiers from crucifying me as well. It would have been easier, in the end, if they had only crucified me instead of Him.

It took only hours for Him to die. I should be grateful for that. It usually took days. I heard Him whisper "Forgive them." I listened as He ministered to the thief, promising Him a place in paradise. How could He still believe in paradise in the midst of hell?

I don't remember how the hours were spent. I was beyond listening, beyond tears, beyond even my faith in the God who created us, who sent His Son, His beloved Son, to die so we could live, so each of us could live — not just now but forever.

Yet even as my heart broke, I found myself whispering "yes."

The Woman at The Well: Living Water

John 4: 5-26 (RSV)

Jesus came to a Samaritan city called Sychar, near the plot of ground that Jacob had given to his son Joseph. Jacob's well was there, and Jesus, tired out by his journey, was sitting by the well. It was about noon.

A Samaritan woman came to draw water, and Jesus said to her, 'Give me a drink'. (His disciples had gone to the city to buy food.) The Samaritan woman said to him, 'How is it that you, a Jew, ask a drink of me, a woman of Samaria?' (Jews do not share things in common with Samaritans.)* Jesus answered her, 'If you knew the gift of God, and who it is that is saying to you, "Give me a drink", you would have asked him, and he would have given you living water.' The woman said to him, 'Sir, you have no bucket, and the well is deep. Where do you get that living water? Are you greater than our ancestor Jacob, who gave us the well, and with his sons and his flocks drank from it?' Jesus said to her, 'Everyone who drinks of this water will be thirsty again, but those who drink of the water that I will give them will never be thirsty. The water that I will give will become in them a spring of water gushing up to eternal life.' The woman said to him, 'Sir, give me this water, so that I may never be thirsty or have to keep coming here to draw water.'

Jesus said to her, 'Go, call your husband, and come back.' The woman answered him, 'I have no husband.' Jesus said to her, 'You are right in saying, "I have no husband"; for you have had five husbands, and the one you have now is not your husband. What you have said is true!'

The woman said to him, 'Sir, I see that you are a prophet. Our ancestors worshipped on this mountain, but you say that the place where people must worship is in Jerusalem.' Jesus said to her, 'Woman, believe me, the hour is coming when you will worship the Father neither on this mountain nor in Jerusalem. You worship what you do not know; we worship what we know, for salvation is from the Jews. But the hour is coming, and is now here, when the true worshippers will worship the Father in spirit and truth, for the Father seeks such as these to worship him. God is spirit, and those who worship him must worship in spirit and truth.' The woman said to him, 'I know that Messiah is coming' (who is called Christ). 'When he comes, he will proclaim all things to us.' Jesus said to her, 'I am he,[*] the one who is speaking to you.'

Just then his disciples came. They were astonished that he was speaking with a woman, but no one said, 'What do you want?' or, 'Why are you speaking with her?'

Then the woman left her water-jar and went back to the city. She said to the people, 'Come and see a man who told me everything I have ever done! He cannot be the Messiah,[*] can he?' They left the city and were on their way to him.

IT WAS JUST AN ORDINARY DAY, like any other day. It was hot. The walk was long. Nothing spectacular. Nothing different from every other day that I came to the well to draw my water. But then I saw Him and nothing was ever ordinary again.

I am a Samaritan woman. He was a Jew. For hundreds of years the Jews have had nothing to do with us. When they saw us on the road, they spat at us and called us "dogs". They hated us and we — we hated them.

It was that day, as I came to the well, that I saw Him sitting there tired, thirsty, and very much alone. It was just about noontime when I approached. Most people came to the well early in the morning or in the cool of the evening. But I, I came when the sun was at its hottest when I knew I would be left alone.

I wanted to be alone, to escape from the stares, the whispered gossip as I walked past, the meddling tongues of the old women. But now there was this stranger. What right did He have to intrude on my only time of peace? I wanted Him gone.

"Who are you?" I shouted. "And why are you here? This is Jacob's well and this is the land of Samaria. You don't belong here."

"And neither do you," He replied softly. "Give me a drink. I thirst."

I was stunned. He wasn't supposed to do that. He wasn't supposed to speak, and certainly not with a tone of respect, not with kindness. I didn't know whether to be insulted or pleased. His request wasn't a demand. It was a question, and when was the last time a man had truly asked me a question, waiting for an answer? When was the last time a man had treated me with respect? I didn't know what to do. How was I supposed to respond?

Normally, when men asked, or just took, I could hide in sarcasm. I would be insulting, defensive. But none of that seemed right this time and I was at a loss. So, I just stood there in silence, staring at Him.

"Give me a drink?" He asked again. "Or, perhaps, just perhaps, I should give you a drink —a drink from my well of living water so you will never be thirsty again."

"Fine. I'll play along," I said. "Give me living water. Then I'll never have to make this long walk again just to haul water back to my tent."

But He wasn't talking about the kind of water I wanted. Or perhaps it was just the water I wanted, the kind of water I longed for. So the conversation went on and on, but I kept feeling as if somehow I was missing the point — just barely missing it but missing it just the same. It's as if He were talking in riddles when all I wanted was a straight answer to a straight question: How could I get some of this living water He kept talking about?

As He talked about water as the source of life and love, I moved the stone away from the well and drew out some of the cold, refreshing water and offered it to Him. He took the gourd from me and took a deep drink. Then He handed it to me with a question in His eyes. Would I take His invitation and drink to life once more? Could I afford to take the risk? I took the chance. I drank from the gourd like a woman who was dying of thirst, and so I was —dying for life and love.

Then He asked the question, and all my hope fled as quickly as it had come. "Go and bring your husband to me." What husband? James, the man with whom I lived, was no husband of mine. In shame, I once more turned away. "I have no husband," I whispered, waiting for the words of scorn, of judgement, that I knew were coming my way. After all, I deserved it. I was no better than a whore.

He didn't condemn me. Almost softly He said to me gently, "You're right. You have had five husbands. Five times you have given your heart and five times you have been betrayed, then divorced.

I knew, just in the sound of His voice, that this man, this Jesus, was not interested in condemning me. Instead He wanted to heal me, to restore my faith in myself and others. He wanted to quench the terrible thirst in my soul for love and acceptance.

I wanted what He was offering more than life itself. I wanted this living water that He spoke of. I wanted to drink from the depth of His love.

As it was for me so long ago, so it is now with you. I can tell that you are thirsty, deep inside, where no one can see the pain and despair. I can tell that you too want to drink from His wellspring of love. Please just ask Him for a drink. I promise you will thirst no more, for His is truly the water of life.

The Bleeding Woman: If I Can Only Touch Him

Luke 8:43-48 (NIV)

A woman was there who had been subject to bleeding for twelve years, but no one could heal her. She came up behind him and touched the edge of his cloak, and immediately her bleeding stopped.

"Who touched me?" Jesus asked. When they all denied it, Peter said, "Master, the people are crowding and pressing against you."

But Jesus said, "Someone touched me; I know that power has gone out from me."

Then the woman, seeing that she could not go unnoticed, came trembling and fell at his feet. In the presence of all the people, she told why she had touched him and how she had been instantly healed. Then he said to her, "Daughter, your faith has healed you. Go in peace."

IF I CAN JUST TOUCH HIM, I will be made well. It is my last hope, my only hope. What is it like to be well? It's been so long that I can't even remember.

Twelve years. Twelve years ago, the bleeding started, and it hasn't stopped. Twelve years of watching my life's blood seep away like water disappearing into the desert sand. Twelve years of isolation and loneliness.

They call me the Bleeding Woman, forgetting that I even have a name. More than anything else, it is the loneliness that wounds. To lose one's blood is curse enough, but to not be able to touch and be touched, that hurts most of all. No man will marry an unclean woman. I will never cradle my own child in my arms. An unclean woman is not allowed even in the sanctuary. To be unclean is to be untouchable, unlovable, inhuman.

Even now it is as if that long-ago moment was this moment — as if it is happening now. I remember saying, "I know if I can just touch Him, I will be made well." I have sacrificed everything to be healed. Physician after physician have taken my money and left me bleeding, their remedies powerless. Even God has forsaken me.

Countless times I have brought two turtle doves and two pigeons to the priest — a sin offering and a guilt offering have been given. Are my offerings unclean too? Will this agony ever be removed from me?

If I can just touch Him, I will be made well.

I sneak up behind Him in the crowd, hoping I won't be recognized as the Bleeding Woman. I follow Him like a wolf stalks a lamb. I shove through the mob, but there are so many people and I am not strong. All I can think is, Get closer. Close enough to touch Him. Suddenly, there is a break in the crowd, and my hand reaches toward His cloak.

If I can just touch Him, I will be made well.

At last my fingers brush against His cloak. I feel the power as it travels up my arm and deep down inside me. Something strange is happening to me. I am drying up! The bleeding has stopped! I am well!

Then the accusation comes. "Who touched me?" He asks. My heart pounds so hard that I am afraid the bleeding will start again. The men with Him say, "There are so many pressing near, who hasn't touched you?" But I know what He means. He means which of the unclean has violated My purity. He means who has taken My power without asking?

I throw myself at His feet, careful not to touch Him this time. "I touched you," I say, "because I am sick and have bled for 12 years. They call me the Bleeding Woman, and I am unclean. I believed that if I just touched You, I would be made well. Please forgive me."

Cowering and trembling, I wait for Him to take back the gift I stole and undo the healing. I wait to hear the words of condemnation I have heard so many times before. I wait for Him to scornfully call me Bleeding Woman, and rush away to wash Himself because He was touched by the unclean. I want to cover my ears but do not.

The crowds close in around us like a noose. They will enjoy hearing Jesus rebuke the Bleeding Woman. He begins, "Daughter…." But there is no condemnation in His voice! He says, "Daughter, your faith has made you well. Go in peace and be healed of your disease."

He reaches down and gently lifts me to my feet, unafraid to touch me. I am feather light in His hands, ready to float away on winds of joy. He will not take back the gift of healing. It is mine to keep, forever. No longer am I Bleeding Woman. Now I am a daughter of the faith able to touch and be touched, love and be loved.

I touched Him, and I was made well.

A Woman: Caught in Adultery

John 8: 2-11 (NIV)

At dawn he appeared again in the temple courts, where all the people gathered around him, and he sat down to teach them. The teachers of the law and the Pharisees brought in a woman caught in adultery. They made her stand before the group and said to Jesus, "Teacher, this woman was caught in the act of adultery. In the Law Moses commanded us to stone such women. Now what do you say?" They were using this question as a trap, in order to have a basis for accusing him.

But Jesus bent down and started to write on the ground with his finger. When they kept on questioning him, he straightened up and said to them, "Let any one of you who is without sin be the first to throw a stone at her." Again, he stooped down and wrote on the ground.

At this, those who heard began to go away one at a time, the older ones first, until only Jesus was left, with the woman still standing there. Jesus straightened up and asked her, "Woman, where are they? Has no one condemned you?" "No one, sir," she said.

"Then neither do I condemn you," Jesus declared. "Go now and leave your life of sin."

I LOVED HIM. He said he loved me. He said his wife was cold. He said his love for her had ended. He said their marriage was a sham, but he did not have the will to divorce her, publicly shame her, leave her with no support. So, he stayed even though he swore his allegiance to me, to our love. And I loved him. I believed him. On one sultry night I gave him my body.

It's true. I committed adultery. But I was not the only one. He too was guilty of the sin. But they let him flee into the break of dawn while they took me from the bed, naked and afraid. They bound my hands so I could not cover myself. They pushed and shoved me through the streets displaying my shame.

We went toward the temple. I was bloody and bruised by the time we got there. I was terrified by then, for I knew what the law said. I knew my punishment would be death, death by stoning. What I did not know was that they were using me and my adultery as a trap for the man who was teaching on the temple steps — teaching a faith of love and forgiveness of sins — teaching a faith of new beginnings — a faith so different from the Pharisees who mocked me and used me as a pawn in their cosmic game.

They shoved me through the crowd and threw me to the ground. They pointed at me and righteously declared that I had sinned — and not an ordinary sin but the sin of adultery — a sin of sex and betrayal. The law of Moses said I must be stoned to death for my crime of passion. We all knew it. The Law was clear. I must die the slow, torturous death of stoning.

They shouted at Him. "What do You say, Jesus? What can You say? You certainly can't disagree with the law of Moses. Yet if You don't, you betray everything You stand for. So what will it be Jesus? Break the Law or kill the woman? What do You say now? Here on the temple steps." You could hear them gloating, "We've got him now. He can't talk Himself out of this one. The law is clear. He'll have no choice but to condemn her."

In the silence that followed, as the crowd held their breath for what would come next, I dared to lift my head toward Him. He looked me in the eyes, but it was not a look of disgust or even condemnation. It was a look of purest love. My heart began to hope even as I bowed in shame before Him, knowing my guilt, knowing my fate.

"We've got you now, Jesus," they shouted. "There is no clever way out for You, no twisting of the meaning of the law. Our faith is black and white. Our actions are either right or wrong. There is no middle way, muddled by this forgiveness You speak of — plead for — every day. There is no room for grace. You are well and truly trapped."

We waited there in silence for Him to reply — for Him to condemn me. In the silence, He walked toward me. He lifted up my head and stared into my pleading countenance. His face was filled with sorrow and something else —something I had forgotten — love. He looked at me with love.

Still, without a word, He stooped down and began to write in the sand by His feet. He just wrote as we all waited. The crowd grew restless. People strained their necks to see. From the back of the crowd I heard them whispering, "What is He writing? What do the words say?"

You could hear them starting to growl. The Pharisees were starting to mutter, but I waited, still and silent for words of forgiveness or death. Which would it be? My fate was in His hands, hands that went on writing in the shifting sand.

As the crowd grew louder, demanding an answer, Jesus stood up. He looked at each of us in turn, His face filled with sorrow. It was as if He saw into the heart of each of us there. Without saying a word, we knew that

He knew what lay in our hearts, what darkness we had each committed.

Finally, He spoke, in a very quiet voice. Softly, He said, "You who are without sin, you throw the first stone."

The Pharisees started to move, but Jesus just stood there silently looking down at the sand. He stooped down again, and again He wrote. They stopped, stood still, read those words, and then, with a look of pure hate, they turned away.

One by one the crowd dropped their stones and left in silence bowed down by their own guilt and shame. At last, no one was left. Jesus knelt down before me, looked me in the eyes once more, and quietly said, "Go. I forgive you. Go — but sin no more." Then He wrapped me in His cloak, still warm with His love, hiding my shame and my nakedness.

It was only then that He turned away. You see, Jesus was not good at throwing stones of judgement, stones of hard words, nor stones of death. And yet, in some ways, His words of love were even harder to bear without breaking your heart. So broken, I stayed there, kneeling in the sand wondering at what had just happened. Then I stood, and said "Yes, Lord. Yes. Thank you. Thank you." And I walked away —not to my old life but to a new one, a life based on the mercy and love I myself had received.

Any time in my life I have been tempted to throw stones of judgement, I have remembered my Lord and his words of grace. I heard again His still, small voice sounding in the depth of my heart, "And you, are you without sin?"

So I give you a stone of your own this day and ask only that you carry it with you. Put it in your pocket — on your kitchen table — wherever you might see it, feel it. And when you are tempted to throw hard words of judgement or condemnation, when you are tempted to throw hard words of gossip or hate, look at that stone, feel its weight in your hand, and ask yourself, what I ask each day, "Are you without sin?" Then listen for the voice of Jesus and lay your stone of anger, bitterness, and petty judgement down. Know His forgiveness and forgive others as well.

Martha: A Friend Who Served

Luke 10: 38-42 (RSV)

As Jesus and his disciples were on their way, he came to a village where a woman named Martha opened her home to him. She had a sister called Mary, who sat at the Lord's feet listening to what he said. But Martha was distracted by all the preparations that had to be made. She came to him and asked, "Lord, don't you care that my sister has left me to do the work by myself? Tell her to help me!"

"Martha, Martha," the Lord answered, "you are worried and upset about many things, but few things are needed—or indeed only one. Mary has chosen what is better, and it will not be taken away from her."

MY NAME IS MARTHA. You know my story. You have probably heard it a hundred times before, but now hear my side of the events that took place that day.

Everyone always wants to be Mary, sitting quietly at the feet of Jesus, listening to him teach, not a worry in the world. Heck, I want to be Mary. But I will now and always will be Martha, but a changed Martha, a quieter, calmer Martha, not so distracted by everything there is to do, yet still aware of my responsibilities and the things that must be done. For there are things that must be done, things that cannot be put off until a later place or time, things of eternal importance.

But let me start at the beginning. My sister, Mary, my brother, Lazarus, and I were all disciples of Jesus, but more than disciples we were friends. Jesus did not have many friends among the throngs that followed Him. Many were attracted by His teachings of love and forgiveness, of acceptance and tolerance, but few really knew Him as we knew Him.

We knew Him when He was dusty and tired from days of teaching and healing. We knew Him when He laughed from sheer joy as a butterfly landed on His nose. We knew Him when he needed rest far from the madding crowd. So our home, my home, became a place of quiet retreat for Him, a place where He could rest, pray, laugh, tell stories, and be free of the demands of ministry. It was the place where His tired, dusty feet could be washed just as He washed the feet of so many.

This was one of those times. He needed to rest before He took up His mantle once again. He needed to relax in comfort with no demands. He needed to be surrounded by friends. So He came to our home.

We did not know He was coming until Andrew came to tell us the day before so we might be ready. It was all such a rush. The house needed cleaning. The meals needed preparing. It was no simple task to prepare to entertain not only Jesus but his closest followers as well. I was determined that he should come and worry about nothing. That was my job — worrying that is. No one else seemed concerned at all but let me tell you they would have been concerned if there was no food to fill their starving bellies and no place to lay their heads!

I swept. I dusted. I fluffed up pillows and made beds. I killed the fatted calf and had a feast ready. I was tired and flustered by the time He arrived and still everything was not ready. I was a woman in motion. I had a list and I was checking it twice when I saw her.

There was Mary sitting quietly there at the feet of Jesus, soaking up His stories, laughing and crying over the adventures they had had on their journey. Well, I had had enough. How dare she do what I longed to do while I was rushing around getting things done. Don't you think I wanted to sit by Jesus and be warmed by His acceptance and love? Don't you think I wanted His hand to rest on my head while I listened quietly as He talked?

Of course, I did! Who wouldn't? Poor me. Poor steadfast Martha. She could be counted on to get things done — to make the beds and be certain the meals were on time. Suddenly I had it. I was tired of all the work and none of the attention. I was tired of being taken for granted. So I took my complaints straight to Jesus.

"Look at her," I said. "She isn't doing a thing. She's just sitting there listening to you while I do all the work." It didn't take a moment for me to know I had said the wrong thing.

She was sitting there, listening to Him. What could be more important than that? In that moment I knew she had taken the better part. It was she that was doing what was necessary. The meal could finish itself. The servants knew what to do.

I didn't really need Jesus to bring the point home. My heart had done a thorough job of it. Yet He did. I think

He did it, not to shame me, but so we could all hear and be reminded of what is truly important. Chasing the butterfly and reveling in God's nature can be just as important —more important —than seeing only the chores and duties piling up around you.

It's not that what I was doing was wrong. Most of it was good and necessary, but when the time came, I failed to relax into love and continued at my own frenzied pace. But don't pretend you don't do it too.

How many times have you gotten frustrated with the work piled up around you while your partner listened to someone pour out her troubles? How often have you told a child "later" when both of you knew "later" would never come? How often have clean floors or a clean desk meant more to you than listening to the stories of Jesus, thinking about them, seeing how to put them to practice in your own life? How often have you missed a time of prayer because of the demands of your schedule, your never-ending list of things to do?

The answer is too many times. You are just as guilty as I am. So Jesus' words are meant for you as much as for me, for we all have more than our share of the Martha I was. Now I've changed. I hope you will too.

Now, instead of getting caught up in my list of things to do, I take the time to listen, to be with Jesus, to know love, to show love. Oh, I still get the necessities done. After all, it would have mattered if there were nothing to eat, but it didn't need to be as elaborate as I once thought. Company comes not because they want to share in a feast but to share with each other — to relax and be renewed. It doesn't matter if dinner is a bowl of soup and a hunk of bread or a five-course meal complete with pressed napkins and shiny silver as long as you are there, completely there, and not chasing your list of things to be checked off.

I will always be Martha — and Mary will always be Mary — but we have both learned to recognize and honor the Martha and Mary in each of us. May you also come to recognize and celebrate the things that are eternal.

Mary Magdalene: The First Witness
John 20:11-18 (RSV)

Now Mary stood outside the tomb crying. As she wept, she bent over to look into the tomb and saw two angels in white, seated where Jesus' body had been, one at the head and the other at the foot. They asked her, "Woman, why are you crying?" "They have taken my Lord away," she said, "and I don't know where they have put him." At this, she turned around and saw Jesus standing there, but she did not realize that it was Jesus. He asked her, "Woman, why are you crying? Who is it you are looking for? "Thinking he was the gardener, she said, "Sir, if you have carried him away, tell me where you have put him, and I will get him." Jesus said to her, "Mary. "She turned toward him and cried out in Aramaic, "Rabboni!" (which means "Teacher"). Jesus said, "Do not hold on to me, for I have not yet ascended to the Father. Go instead to my brothers and tell them, 'I am ascending to my Father and your Father, to my God and your God.'" Mary Magdalene went to the disciples with the news: "I have seen the Lord!" And she told them that he had said these things to her.

MY NAME IS MARY. I grew up in Magdala, a famous port city on the Sea of Galilee. Magdala was known for fun and good times — a place where anything goes.

My parents were well off and gave me everything I ever wanted — except for time — except for love. I grew up with this ache in my heart, this emptiness in my soul to be loved by someone — anyone.

So I began to sleep around, thinking that the more men who loved me the more I would feel loved. Then I turned to buying things — jewelry, perfume, clothes. You name it. I bought it. I thought that the more things I owned the happier I would be.

When none of that worked, I turned to drugs and alcohol. Not because I wanted to, not even because they made me happy, but because, at least for a while, I wouldn't feel anything at all. The pain in my heart would be numbed and I wouldn't dream of what it would be like if someone loved me — if I could only love myself. My life felt empty, senseless, the days seemed grey with hopelessness and I was on the verge of suicide when I heard about this Jesus.

They said He was coming to Magdala to teach and I knew I had to see Him. They said He was a miracle worker and I thought perhaps He could work a miracle in my life. After all, they said He had turned water into wine, that He healed the sick, that He had even raised a man from the dead. I had to go see Him for myself even though I knew He was probably just another fake or one of those crazy prophets claiming to be sent by God.

So I went, and it was as if He looked through the crowd, straight into my heart. It felt as if He knew all about me — the drugs, the sex, all of it and that He loved me in spite of it all. In those few moments, it was as if all the sadness in my heart, all the pain I had carried throughout my life, were gone.

He didn't love me because of my appearance, my money, my family status. None of that mattered to Him. I was the one who was important. The real me — the me God created me to be. I knew I needed to follow Him wherever He might go.

So I left Magdala and started to travel with Him to learn from Him. He told us the most marvelous stories about the kingdom of God — stories that I still learn from, but more important than anything He said was how He lived His life. He loved everyone without judgment. He seemed to have a special place in His heart for those whom no one else could love — the outcast, the sinners — as well as the saints. I was drawn to that love and slowly but surely, I learned to love as well. I remember, too, how as we traveled along the way, He would stop, just to look at a flower or listen to a babbling brook. It was as if He drew strength from even the smallest gifts of God.

There were also times when we would drop back from the crowd and He would talk to me — just me. I felt whole and wonderful, as if anything were possible.

Perhaps, then, you can understand just a bit of how I felt during that last week in Jerusalem. It started as I had always dreamed. He rode into town to cries of Hosanna, and He spent the week teaching at the temple, but then, one night, Passover night, the priests came to arrest Him even as He was praying in the garden.

They beat and mocked Him and sent Him to Pilate for trial. I pushed through the crowds to see Him as I had never seen Him before. Gone was the man I loved and in His place was this bruised and battered person. The crowds started to yell "Crucify Him. Crucify Him."

I couldn't understand what had happened. These were the same men and women who had cried out Hosanna just a few days ago. "Stop it!" I cried. "Stop it." But still they yelled those terrible words "Crucify Him."

I followed them to the hill of Calvary where they laid Him on the ground and pounded His hands and His feet into the wood of the cross. I was there as they gambled for his cloak — the only thing He had left. I was there with my heart breaking until He finally said, "It is finished". As He died, all the hope and dreams, love and life, within me died as well, crucified on that cross with Him.

I stood there watching as they took His body from the cross. I was there as they carried Him to the tomb. I was there when they lay His body on that cold grey slab of rock. I was there as they rolled the stone in front of the grave. I was there, even though it felt as if I had died inside.

I had to do something. I had to care for Him even now, so I went on that first Sunday to wrap His body in the herbs and spices that would give Him a decent burial. But when I got there the stone was rolled away and I knew — I just knew — they had stolen His body.

Suddenly I could take it no more. They had stolen everything from me — and now they had stolen even His body from me too. I was so hopeless, so weighed down with grief, and suddenly I started to cry with all the pent-up tears of the last horrific days. I couldn't stop crying.

Finally, through my tears I looked inside the grave and I saw two men there — at least they looked like men. They said to me "Why do you weep?" And all I could say was, "Where have you taken Him?" There was no answer. Then I saw the gardener and ran to Him, falling at His feet, begging Him, "Please I said, where have you taken him? Let me see him even now. Give me as much as that."

Then I heard it, the voice I would never forget. His voice, full of caring and love. "Mary." It was all He needed to say. "Rabboni! Teacher!" All the joy in heaven and earth were tied up in those words.

I couldn't believe it. He was alive. He was dead no more. He had risen from the grave to show me and to show you that His love, His power, His strength is greater than anything evil can do.

He is alive for me still in this moment and He can be alive within you as well, for He loves you with an undying love. That is what I really need to tell you. It is a story of love and power -- a story of the Son of God the true messiah. He has come for you just as He has for me. Decide to follow Him now, today. Stand with me as we tell His story to the nations as all His disciples have told it throughout the ages.

CPSIA information can be obtained
at www.ICGtesting.com
Printed in the USA
LVHW042339010719
622901LV00011B/33/P